ELIMINATING
ANXIETY
FOREVER

Watch Your Worries Disappear
Like A Cloud of Smoke

Crystal Barton

Table of Contents

Chapter 1:

A Guided Journal For Anxiety

Anxiety is the silent killer.

Anxiety is a state of worry when you are unsure about the next step. Very few people know how to handle anxiety when they face it. Instead, they bury their heads in the sand and hope that things will eventually work themselves out.

What remains unclear are the disastrous results of actions resulting from anxiety. Healthy relationships have collapsed when partners succumbed to anxiety, job opportunities have been lost, and once-in-a-lifetime chances have slipped from our hands because we were unable to contain the anxiety that was building in us.

We will lose count of the much that anxiety has cost us. Sometimes, it has been misconstrued as a "normal" feeling and nothing is done to tame it. That is the moment the rain starts beating us. Nothing much can be done when we realize the damage anxiety has done in our lives.

Here is a guided journal for anxiety:

Take A Step Back

Sometimes we are anxious because we do not understand what we are into. We get nervous about new experiences and do not know how to proceed from there. Our judgment is often clouded when we are in unfamiliar territories. The fear of not being right builds anxiety in us and we want to please everybody. What a herculean task!

Take a step back to get the bigger picture. This will bring clarity because you can look at all variables at once and weigh them, one after another. Moving back gives you a sense of power and control when you realize it was not that difficult in the first place. You will be more comfortable in an environment you can manipulate.

Anxiety results from the fear of the unknown. When you withdraw a little from a situation, you can comfortably evaluate it because nobody will judge you.

Take Off Your Mind from The Subject Matter

This is an evasion strategy. You are not always required to face your fears immediately. It is okay to withdraw your attention when you are anxious about something or an unprecedented condition. You will live to tackle it another day. Do not pressure yourself to act within a deadline. The timeframes you confine yourself within will haunt you especially when you feel inadequate for what is ahead of you.

Put your mind on things that bring you solace and calm to fight the anxiety. You understand yourself better than anyone does and you are best placed to make this decision. Think about your dream car – Rolls-Royce, Ferrari, Porsche, Chevrolet, or any other that fascinates you. Relaxing thoughts will calm you down and kick away anxiety.

Our comfort zones give us confidence because we can handle ourselves better in them. Anxiety cannot win the battle when we are in them.

Do Not Think Of Any Consequences – There Are None

There are no consequences of acting right. What gives anxiety room to thrive is the fear of consequences that will befall us if we do not act expectedly. Deny anxiety the pleasure of tormenting you by not accepting liability for doing the right thing.

Even in situations that present a dilemma, choose to do the right thing over the popular choice. Populism is not always right, and its consequences are unavoidable. They will finally come to haunt you. To be safe, make the right choice whose consequences are positive and will bring you honor.

Regardless of how quickly you will want to work on your anxiety and make a popular choice, its results are indelible. Purpose to cure anxiety through the right channel with positive consequences.

Consult Widely

Consultations are the preserve of the wise. Only the wise accept that they do not have a monopoly of ideas. They seek the opinions of other people who could have had a similar experience. When you find yourself in a compromising situation, remember that you are not the first person to experience the same. Someone else has been there and they made it.

Anxiety grows in ignorance. You get nervous because you do not know how to handle the challenge your way. Seek the advice of experienced people and they will guide you on how to navigate unchartered territories.

In conclusion, anyone could be anxious. What makes the difference is how different people handle it. Some turn it into an opportunity for growth while others allow it to kill their dreams. Make the right choice.

Chapter 2:

Health Anxiety for Women

Anxiety is a normal stress response. However, it can become harmful when it becomes difficult to control and influence your daily life. Anxiety disorders affect nearly 1 in 5 adults in the United States. Women are more than twice as likely as men to develop an anxiety disorder during their lifetime. Anxiety disorders are often treated with counselling, medications, or a combination of the two. Some women also find yoga or meditation to help with anxiety disorders.

Anxiety is a feeling of fret, nervousness, or fear about an event or situation. This is a normal stress response. This will help you pay attention in challenging situations at work, study harder for an exam, or focus on an important speech. It will help you deal with it in general. However, if the anxiety interferes with your daily life, fear of everyday activities that are not threatening, such as taking a bus or talking to a coworker, may make the anxiety go away. Anxiety can also be a sudden terrorist attack without a threat.

From an early age, girls are more likely to suffer from anxiety disorders than boys. In fact, by the age of six, girls are diagnosed with an anxiety disorder. This difference persists through adolescence and adulthood when twice as many women as men suffer from anxiety disorders. Girls were six times more likely to develop a generalized anxiety disorder. Boys had higher levels of OCD before puberty. Women were more likely to have panic disorder, GAD, agoraphobia, and post-traumatic stress disorder. Women are twice as likely to have phobias as men. There are minor gender differences in social anxiety and obsessive-compulsive disorder.

Types Of Anxiety Disorders:

1. Generalized Anxiety Disorder

People with GAD worry too much about everyday health, money, work, and family problems. With GAD, your mind often goes to the worst-case scenario, even when you have little or no reason to worry. Women with GAD can worry about getting through the day. They may have muscle tension and other stress-related physical symptoms, such as trouble sleeping or an upset stomach. Sometimes anxiety prevents people with GAD from performing everyday tasks. Women with GAD have a higher risk of depression and other anxiety disorders than men with GAD. They are also more likely to have a family history of depression.

2. Panic Disorder

Panic disorder is twice as common in women as in men. People with panic disorder suddenly feel fear when there is no real danger. Panic attacks can cause feelings of unrealism, fear of impending doom, or fear of losing control. Fear of physical symptoms that one cannot explain is also a sign of panic disorder. People with panic attacks sometimes think they have a heart attack, lose consciousness, or die.

3. Social Phobia

Social phobia, also known as social anxiety disorder, is diagnosed when people are very anxious and shy in everyday social situations. People with social phobia are afraid of being viewed and judged by others. They can panic easily and often experience panic attacks.

4. Obsessive-Compulsive Disorder (OCD)

People with obsessive-compulsive disorder have unwanted thoughts (obsessions) or behaviours (compulsions) that cause anxiety. They may keep checking the oven or iron or repeat the same procedure to control the stress that these thoughts cause. Often, consciousness eventually comes to prevent a person.

Treatment

1. Psychotherapy

The most common treatment for health problems is psychotherapy, specifically cognitive behavioral therapy (CBT). CBT can be very effective in treating health problems because it teaches you skills that will help you cope with your disability. CBT can participate as an individual or as a group. Some of the benefits of CBT include:

- Identifies your health concerns and beliefs.
- Explore other ways to change your mind and see how your body feels.
- Raise awareness of how your worries affect you and your behaviour and react differently to body sensations and symptoms.
- Learn to better deal with anxiety and stress.
- Learn to stop avoiding situations and actions because of your bodily sensations.
- You are avoiding physical examinations for signs of illness and seeking confirmation that you are consistently healthy.
- Improve your skills at home, at work or school, on social media and with others.
- Check for other mental health conditions, such as depression or bipolar disorder.

Other forms of psychotherapy are also sometimes used to treat health problems. This may include behavioural stress management and exposure therapy. If your symptoms are severe, your doctor may recommend medications along with other treatments.

2. Medication

If psychotherapy alone improves health problems, this is usually all used to treat your condition. However, some people do not respond to psychotherapy. If this applies to you, your doctor can recommend a drug. Antidepressants such as Selective Serotonin Reuptake Inhibitors (SSRIs) are often used for this condition. If you have a mood or anxiety disorder in addition to anxiety, drugs used to treat these conditions may help. Some medications for health problems have severe risks and side effects. It is important to discuss treatment options with your doctor carefully.

Chapter 3:

7 Steps for Health Anxiety Recovery

Even when you're healthy, that controlled worry about your health is normal. However, if such concerns become uncontrollable, you may have developed health anxiety. Health anxiety can affect anyone, whether they are healthy or have an existing health condition. In extreme cases, health anxiety will cause you a great deal of distress and, however, adversely affect your daily life or things you love and your relationships. The plain fact about health anxiety is that it causes an irrational fear of severe health conditions. As a result, any physical symptoms, even normal bodily functions, frequently cause health concerns. A burn or pimple on your body. Could it be Skin cancer? Sweating at night. Could it be HIV or lymphoma? Headaches? You already know it isn't a brain tumor! You might well be having a lot of negative or scary ideas right now. However, every situation is backed with ample remedies or mitigations.

Here are 7 steps for health anxiety recovery.

1. Learn More About Anxiety

The first step toward recovery is to acquire every bit of information relating to anxiety in general. That is, studying the physiology of the body's reaction to anxiety triggers. You'll discover that in most anxiety cases, such bodily reactions are typically caused by relatively harmless circumstances. It is, therefore, essential that you learn ways that will promote control over such reactions.

2. Seek Cognitive-Behaviour Therapy

CBT is a type of therapy that focuses on your cognition, how you think, and your behaviours. It is rooted from the notion that the type of emotions you feel whenever you are facing a certain situation influences how you respond and behave. CBT involves altering the patterns of your thinking and opinions that cause anxiety and coaching you to confront your fears to desensitize you. It enables you to train yourself to approach the fear factor that triggers anxiety.

3. Shift Your Focus

A person who suffers from health anxiety usually concentrates more on how the body functions. The more you concentrate on how your body functions, the more you'll notice physical sensations. As a result, you're most likely to develop worrying thoughts of physical symptoms. In such cases, divert your attention to something else to distract yourself from the troubling thoughts.

4. Exercise Mindfulness

Practicing mindfulness is the art of feeling your present self, that is being in the moment and allowing your body to feel the situation as it is. It further entails paying attention to the present moment and disconnecting from unhelpful thoughts. While the practice has its roots in meditation, it has found increasing use in therapy. Mindfulness-based cognitive and behavioural is highly effective for people suffering from health anxiety.

5. Avoid Google-Searching Your Symptoms

If you already have health anxiety, Google is not your friend. Avoid using Google to look up the causes of what you physically feel because this will only make your worries worse. A distressing thought is a channel for imagining the worst-case scenarios. You must maintain a balanced perspective on your situation.

6. Practice Cognitive Diffusion

Thoughts are only perceptions and should not be used to establish your reality. When you ruminate, you start to believe that your thoughts reflect your reality. For instance, a person with health anxiety who often worries about their heart may think they have a heart condition when a physical symptom arises. When you practice cognitive diffusion, you can identify and challenge your negative thought, allowing you to reframe them.

7. Work With What Works for You

It's normal to feel overwhelmed when you try out a technique that has been successful to several people, and it turns out to be conflicting. It unsurprising that not every remedy is relevant for everyone experiencing health anxiety disorder. This is because each person is affected differently. You'll want to find what works best for your specific case, which may necessitate a few trials and errors.

Conclusion

Like other anxiety disorders, health anxiety can be daunting to your whole existence. You find yourself constantly worrying about getting sick or falling ill. You frequently get concerned about any physical symptoms you are experiencing and what they may mean. If health-related feelings, concerns, and thoughts begin to dominate your daily life, it may be time to take action.

Chapter 4:

7 Signs of Social Anxiety

It is a well-known fact that the times we're living in today are fraught with unprecedented anxiety. But eventually we find ways to bounce back like nothing happened. Even so, there are certain anxious patterns in your life that you might need extra help to break. If you feel overly uncomfortable, or stressed with the mere thought of social situations that you avoid social gatherings at all costs, you might have social anxiety disorder.

Social anxiety according to mayo clinic is a "social phobia," or fear that causes avoidance of social events or situations in fear of being judged by others. It is based on the notion that you might do or say something within the context of social interactions and end up embarrassing or humiliating yourself. On that account, you develop a deep and sometimes irrational fear of being judged or rejected by others.

Here are 7 signs of social anxiety.

1. You've Had This Feeling Ever Since You Were A Teen

The Diagnostic and Statistical Manuals define social anxiety disorder as a time limit. You must have felt this way for six months to be eligible. However, scientists have discovered that the average age at which social anxiety manifests itself is around 13, with most cases occurring between the ages of 11 and 19. This is the period when you're most self-conscious because your adolescent brains are usually more sensitive to other people's reactions. It's pretty uncommon for a social anxiety disorder to manifest after 25, so you might be okay if you've made it that far.

2. You're Overly Sensitive to Criticism

Being criticized doesn't settle well for anyone, and it is incredibly distressing when you have a social anxiety disorder. That's because what you always dread is coming true. Since you are constantly worried about being rejected or judged by others, social anxiety makes you overly sensitive to everything critical, criticizing, or ridiculing. It even prevents you from seizing a possible opportunity because you're constantly looking for failure or humiliation.

3. Self-Esteem Issues

It is common knowledge that many nervous disorders are correlated to self-esteem issues, and social anxiety is not exempt. Studies show that many psychological disorders such as body image issues, fear, and frustration are closely linked to this disorder. The greater your social anxiety, the lower your self-esteem.

4. You Are Self-Conscious

Recent studies show that highly impaired people with social anxiety lack strong social networks. As Thomas Rodebaugh, puts it, "social anxiety makes you think you are coming across much worse than you are." They are always self-conscious and miscalculating how badly they appear in relationships or friendships and might even pass up a job opportunity in fear of being rejected or singled out as a failure.

5. Extreme Physical Symptoms of Anxiety

Social anxiety disorder manifests itself in your thoughts and your body. Panic attacks and anxiety become severe and frequent when you encounter a social situation or do something you regret. The Mayo Clinic lists the physical symptoms to include: Sweating, shortness of breath, muscle tension, fast heart rate, a desire to run, dizziness, nausea, and becoming blank. The symptoms are typically your body's response to fear or a genuine upsetting feeling.

6. You Turn to Substance Abuse for Normal Functionality

Research has proven a high correlation between alcohol or drug misuse and social phobia. The severity of social phobia can sometimes reach a point where sufferers resort to substance abuse. That is, you need drugs to feel comfortable or function properly. If you're always in dire need of drinking or smoking a joint before any social event and feeling guilty later, it's a sign.

7. You Fear Asking Anything in Public

When you're a person who suffers a lot in public, this is a sentimental sign that you could be suffering from a social anxiety. Of course, people with social anxiety disorder are hesitant to ask for simple things, such as food or just anything in public places. Even in places where no one knows you, you still feel this way.

Conclusion

It is okay to feel shy or thrilled before or during a social event. However, if the thought of being social or being in a social setting creates terror within you, something is wrong. You might consider seeking help.

Chapter 5:

Mindfulness Over Anxiety

Anxiety The Thief!

You may not realize it until the moment it steals your joy. Anxiety is the modern-day thief that deprives people of their joy. It camouflages behind various excuses but finally reveals its true colors. It is just a matter of time.

Anxiety instills worry for no good reason. All of a sudden you start to think 'what if things go wrong' when nothing has happened yet. This mentality will lie that you are planning ahead while the reality is that you are overstretching your ability. There is only so much that you can control.

Cheat Anxiety Today!

When you are anxious about something, your body will naturally respond to your fears. You tend to breathe a little faster than the normal rate, some people will sweat in their palms, and you will be absent-minded. Your mind will wander to how you can rescue yourself from the fix you find yourself in.

You can overcome anxiety in two ways: the short way and the long durable one.

The shorter way is regulating your basal metabolic rate. Here is what you should do whenever you are anxious. Inhale and exhale slowly paying attention to only the flow of air into and out of your lungs. Close your eyes as you do this.

Repeating this procedure will calm you down, your breathing rate will return to normal and you will regain your composure in a while.

While you may have beaten anxiety at the moment, you need a durable solution for it.

Mindfulness It Is!

Mindfulness is prioritizing logic over emotions no matter how strong they may be. Whenever you are anxious, tell yourself "Mindfulness over anxiety."

It happens in several ways but here are proven ways to overcome anxiety:

1. Take Caution

Most people throw caution to the wind about other matters except their cause for anxiety.

This is a dangerous trend because instead of curing anxiety, it will shift it elsewhere. Solving one problem only to create another is a cycle you will not want to be in.

Since anxiety is caused by worry, when you are careful about what you do there will be no cause for worry because you will ensure what is in your control unfolds just fine. Tie any loose ends to your plans to reduce risk and you will not have to worry about mishaps.

2. Build Healthy Relationships

You are probably anxious about somebody else's reaction because the both of you have not bonded well. This gives room to insecurities – a very unhealthy component of relationships.

It is difficult to be anxious about people that do not matter. The people you love and care for the most are the ones responsible for your anxiety.

Endeavor to build healthy relationships with them so that you can be confident of expressing yourself to them on anything, whether good or bad.

Healthy relationships are our refuge even during anxious moments and they should not be the very cause of our trouble.

3. Nourishing Your Mind

You should constantly feed your mind with the right things. Failure to do this, our fears take root and it becomes difficult to remove them.

Read widely and fill your mind with knowledge. Expand your expertise in science, astronomy, and whatever interests you. This will give no room for fear and anxiety to thrive.

Moreover, you can come up with solutions to what causes anxiety if you have the right skills. We are anxious when we are helpless. Having the knowledge to 'rescue' ourselves from such moments is good because we will always be in charge.

4. Planning To Reduce Risk

Uncertainty is what causes anxiety. The future is a gamble and not everything is guaranteed. When you plan, you will feel more secure and so will the people you are with. There will be surety about many things that would have otherwise cost you sleepless nights.

Mindfulness over anxiety includes these four and many other steps to curb anxiety before it even sprouts. You shall eventually emerge victoriously.

Chapter 6:

10 Ways To Stop Anxiety

Everyone experiences some anxious moments in their busy lives. Anxiety is, in fact, scientifically proven as the most common mental health issue. It may not be a cause for concern on the one hand, but it may be detrimental to you, on the other hand. Anxiety interferes with your ability to make decisions, hence preventing you from having a normal life.

Being anxious and dealing with it is never easy. The ability to handle anxiety is a long-term process that doesn't happen spontaneously. However, there are various techniques that have been proven effective when incorporated into your daily routine. When anxiety is a little over the top, consider the following management strategies.

Here are 10 ways to stop anxiety.

1. Meditation

Meditation is proven to be an excellent way of reducing anxiety and enhancing your intuition, lowering blood pressure, and increasing your focus. Meditating calms anxious thoughts and reduces the body's reaction to such unpleasant feelings. Take a break and practice a meditation ritual; you can go for a jog, do yoga, take deep breaths, or do other relaxation techniques. Relaxing or calming your body is proven to develop your mind-set, or the "inner game," essential for your mental health.

2. Treat the Underlying Cause of Stress

In addition to temporarily alleviating anxiety symptoms, consider looking into the root causes. Create a checklist of what you're in control of and those you can't. Then, put your focus on addressing issues you can control. For instance, if your debts keep you awake at night, devise a strategy to solve them. Turn your anxious thoughts into productive action whenever possible.

3. Understand Your Fear

Merely trying to suppress your anxious thoughts may worsen your situation. Persuading yourself not to think about it is likely to rebound. The widely publicized "white bear experiment" in 1987 highlighted this perplexing impact where the respondents admitted to seeing more 'white bears.' Just accept that you are anxious, and that your extraneous thoughts will eventually go away.

4. Schedule Time for Your Feelings

Have you had a great deal of smoldering embers to extinguish? Consider setting time for the burning thoughts. Yes, it will appear to be illogical. Start by adding 'thinking time to your to-do list. Transitioning simply reacting to whatever comes your way to strategizing for your prospective future lessens your day-to-day fires and enables you to optimize what is pertinent.

5. Redefine Your Unreal Beliefs

Anxiety can lead to catastrophic predictions. Picturing your entire future being ruined by one unfortunate mistake or that one bad grade will leave you restless and will eventually fuel anxiety. Replace exaggeratedly negative statements with more realistic ones. When you find yourself imagining the worst-case scenario about a situation, constantly remind yourself that even if you mess up, it won't be the end.

6. Switch It Up

If you can't get your mind off from worrying, and if the situation is beyond your control, engage your body with something new. You can take a walk or clean your closet-whatever it takes to keep your mind occupied. Focusing your attention somewhere else, even for a few minutes, can help reduce your stress and pave a way for a much needed break your mind may need.

7. Start a Gratitude Journey

Do it every night; it works and its simple. Learn to appreciate the little things in your life. You can also keep a journal to write about your worrying moments and the steps you can take to overcome them.

8. Talk to Someone

Getting together with family and friends, even strangers at Starbucks, and talking about how you're feeling can be beneficial. If opening up is hard for you, consider other avenues like jotting it down or other online platforms.

9. Find A Quiet Space

Sights and sounds can frequently amplify a panic attack. Find a peaceful place to vent to whenever you feel anxious. Venting in a quiet place allows you to create a safer place for your mind, making it easier to practice mindfulness and other coping strategies.

10. Stay Away From Alcohol

Because alcohol is a natural sedative, it often takes the edge off first. However, research indicates a link between anxiety and alcohol consumption, with coexisting anxiety disorders and alcohol use disorder (AUD). Excessive consumption of alcohol interferes with your serotine levels which is also responsible for your mental health. Such imbalances often stimulate symptoms of anxiety in your body.

Conclusion

Anxiety is not a cause for alarm in most cases, but if left untreated, it can develop into a disorder that has a negative impact on your mental health. Consider the above anxiety management techniques whenever you feel anxious. And also, remember to seek professional help when needed.

Chapter 7:

Rid Yourself of Anxiety

What is it like living with an unknown fear, dread, restlessness, and nervousness? Seems odd and inappropriate. However, many of us are familiar with and face such emotions almost every day or occasionally. Your bad experiences, any loss you suffered, and traumas in past, triggers those anxious emotions.

Stressing over ordinary things like work, school, finances, and relationships is the most common cause of anxiety for most of us. Whenever you take on too much stress and pressure about something, you become more anxious. The more anxious you are, the more depressed and stressed you become about little things.

Sometimes this anxiety puts you in an embarrassing situation. You react weirdly when you have intense stress about little things.

Exaggerating things, pessimistic thinking, and overthinking play a vital role in anxiety and simply leads to depression and psychological distress. You become unable to concentrate, your thoughts become clouded and leave you with no direction. While we all experience normal anxiety during stressful situations, some people suffer from anxiety disorders and worry about minor things constantly and unnecessarily.

An average amount of anxiety can sometimes be beneficial. It can improve concentration and learning. In addition, it causes us to get anxious when we have an important task to complete or exams at school to prepare for. The stress of these things keeps you focused and alert. Fortunately, once the task is finished, this anxiety abates. But if this anxiety extends for a long period, it can affect your ability to learn and concentrate. In this situation, the brain shuts down so it cannot process, making the task more difficult.

It isn't worth it to try to achieve anything in life while you're stressed out. To succeed in life, you'll need to let go of this stress. So, what should you do to rid yourself of anxiety? Keep in mind that it is all in our heads. We control our emotions, thoughts, and feelings. As humans, we have all the power to control our lives. We just need to realize it.

Take charge of your life and make quick decisions. Don't spend hours thinking about little things like what to eat today? Or what to wear? As we strive for perfection in everything, we not only exhaust our time, but also limit our ability to make decisions, and sometimes, we even end up doing nothing, which is how we develop anxiety.

High standards and unrealistic expectations can also cause anxiety. And when you cannot reach that standard or accomplish it, you feel demotivated and think you are not able to achieve anything in life. That's where you start stressing. It causes a fear inside you, that always keeps you from the beginning, and you put things off for tomorrow; tomorrow that never comes. Don't try to accomplish everything at once. Take small steps and don't run over perfection. You don't need to wait for the perfect time, if you have the skills, just go for it now, without worrying whether it's good or bad, just go for it. It makes things easier for you if you want to accomplish something.

Living a risk-taking lifestyle gives you a sense of empowerment. This sense of freedom and courage replaces your anxiety, and you feel delighted doing everything. Take a chance on yourself and don't think too much. Trust yourself and believe in your abilities. With the right motivation and an optimistic outlook, you can accomplish anything in life.

Chapter 8:

The Battle Against Anxiety And Depression

The Loop of Life

We cannot help to be worried about this or that. Solving one problem gives birth to another complex one. This is the cycle we have to deal with. You may think that enough money can solve your problems. Once you have it, another one pops up.

Power too cannot solve your problems. It can only facilitate so much and after that you are alone. Ask those in power how much they crave privacy. Their lives are in constant public scrutiny. Consider the British monarch. The movement of members of the royal family is under constant watch. Even their private lives literally involve the whole world.

This is how our lives are in a loop. If you do not watch out, anxiety and depression will be your daily dose. They can never be fully eliminated but can be kept under control.

Be The Master

The master is the one in charge at all times. When he does not have things under control, he ceases being the master. Similarly, take charge of your life. Control what is within your reach and let not exterior factors affect your lifestyle. This is how you can be in charge:

1. Do Not Succumb To Peer Pressure

Do not compare your lives with your peers and feel inferior to them. Your destinies are different as is your personality.

Social media has not made things any better. Almost everything is about competition. Everyone wants fame and success. It is astonishing the lengths that people can go for social media clout. When they fail to match the fake competition, depression sets in.

You are unique in your own way even if you do not belong to the 'class' of your peers. Do not compare yourself with anyone.

2. Understand Time and Seasons

Everyone has their destined time and season to shine. Do not be anxious about anything. Find comfort that your time for glory has not yet arrived.

In due time, the world shall see you shine.

You may be worried that time is not on your side. Your colleagues could have their own businesses, yet you have none. They could also be married while you are hardly in any serious relationship.

All such thoughts of comparison are uncalled for. Your time has not yet come. Trust in destiny as you work your way up the ladder of life. Cheer them and be happy for their success. Do not wallow in your pity.

3. Find A Hobby

A hobby is something that you love. You can do it for hours without getting fed up. It could be singing, writing, swimming, playing soccer, or cooking. Identify your hobby and spend as much time as possible doing it.

Your hobby will capture your time and attention. You will be occupied having fun and will worry less about things you cannot control. Hobbies are powerful drivers of motivation too. They can help you rediscover your joy and open a new chapter.

4. Find A Support Partner

You need a support partner in your battle against anxiety. Someone you will pour your heart to when you have no one to turn to. Depression can make you lose your senses. Someone needs to be there to help you restore your sanity.

A support partner can be a parent, spouse, or best friend. They should be understanding and preferably someone you can completely trust with your deepest secrets. You should keep nothing away from them.

Their help does not make you any weaker. Instead, you are forming a strong team against a common enemy – depression.

5. Seek Medical Help

The good news is that it is never too late to seek medical attention even after it has badly affected you. Something can be done about it.

The earlier you seek treatment, the better your chances of coming out of it safely.

You shall eventually prevail against anxiety and depression.

Chapter 9:

Mental Health for Women

Mental health and empowerment are two essential needs for a woman. This is because being a woman makes you more susceptible to unique mental health risks, and seeking help, considering your personality can be too stigmatizing. Evidence suggests that almost two times compared to men, women are more likely to experience mental health problems like depression, anxiety, post-traumatic stress disorder(PTSD), and eating disorders.

You're more likely to experience both physical and emotional stress during Your major life transitions such as pregnancy, motherhood, and menopause. Your mental well-being is more so affected by economic and social strains such as poverty, infertility, perinatal loss, abuse, unemployment, and isolation, increasing the likelihood of depression. What makes a woman more vulnerable to mental health problems?

Here is mental health for women.

1. Is Gender a Factor to Mental Issues?

Biological causes, according to mental health studies, take part in the development of women's mental problems. The reality is, as a woman, your serotonin levels are lower than those of men, making you more likely to experience mood swings. As a result, you're more susceptible to hormonal changes and, subsequently, mental health issues.

2. Some Influences on Women's Mental Issues

Women are heavily affected by sociocultural influences and values, which leads to depression and anxiety. The societal realities have kept women as primary caregivers-raising children and taking up household roles. Even though gender roles have shifted, where you see men as caregivers and women taking more powerful jobs, a significant number of women still face it.

It's no surprise that females get sexualized through social media, movies, TV shows, among others. According to the American Psychological Association, such practices can interfere with your self-esteem and negate on your body image. Further, a woman is more likely to be sexually abused. These factors cause depression, anxiety, guilt, which are detrimental to your mental health.

3. Women's Mental Issues

Depression for women can manifest itself in various ways, including both mental and physical symptoms. You're likely to experience depression in different stages of your life, divided into premenstrual, perinatal, and premenopausal. It could be due to the changing hormone estrogen projected on your body and its influence on your brain function and stress response.

Pre-Menstrual Syndrome

Premenstrual syndrome (PMS) is very common among women, but a small number of women experience symptoms of premenstrual dysphoric disorder (PMDD). Signs and symptoms are; depression, mood swings, anger, anxiety, feeling overwhelmed, difficulty concentrating, and tension. Studies show that ant-depressants working on your sensory receptors can play a significant role in managing it.

Relationship Between Depression and Pregnancy

When considering the relationship between pregnancy and depression, even though this is the time you celebrate thrive and glow, a few women silently suffer from depression and anxiety. Untreated depression can be harmful to you and your unborn child. Therefore, it should not be ignored, and professional psychiatric assessment is mandatory. There are also a few medications that can be used during pregnancy and breastfeeding if it becomes vital to it treat medically at that point in time.

Post-Natal Depression

The topic on post-natal depression is very important, because it's actually treated as a common phenomenon. The chances of experiencing post-natal depression are high if you've had an episode or two episodes of depression in the past. Post-natal depression is usually mislabelled as an everyday experience or an adjustment of childbirth because of ignorance and lack of awareness. To the contrary and close to it is "baby blues." In the first two weeks, post-delivery, you can experience being anxious, cheerful, and feeling down, which often get better as you adjust to the process.

Perimenopause Depression

Multiple studies link perimenopause to depression and anxiety. The period slightly before you enter the menopause is marked as a phase of mood swings and more depressive symptoms. Feeling depressed during premenopausal years is usually conceived as standard, and most of the time, you might be forced to adopt it as a common phenomenon. However, it's always wise to seek assistance whenever you experience depression or anxiety during this phase.

Conclusion

If you or someone under your care are experiencing mental health problems, don't wait to seek help or treatment whatsoever. Knowledge is power, and so is empowerment. The sooner you mitigate your underlying conditions, the better because at the end of the day, the goal is to make most of your life. There is no such a thing as the right time to seek help, and nor can you justify being afraid or embarrassed as a ground for your mental health problems.

Chapter 10:

Choose Getting into Nature for Better Mood and Happiness

It's clear that hiking—and any physical activity—can reduce stress and anxiety. But, there's something about being in nature that may augment those impacts.

In one recent experiment conducted in Japan, participants were assigned to walk either in a forest or in an urban center (taking walks of equal length and difficulty) while having their heart rate variability, heart rate, and blood pressure measured. The participants also filled out questionnaires about their moods, stress levels, and other psychological measures.

Results showed that those who walked in forests had significantly lower heart rates and higher heart rate variability (indicating more relaxation and less stress) and reported better moods and less anxiety than those who walked in urban settings. The researchers concluded that there's something about being in nature that had a beneficial effect on stress reduction, above and beyond what exercise alone might have produced. In another study, researchers in Finland found that urban dwellers who strolled for as little as 20 minutes through an urban park or woodland reported significantly more stress relief than those who strolled in a city center.

The reasons for this effect are unclear, but scientists believe that we evolved to be more relaxed in natural spaces. In a now-classic laboratory experiment by Roger Ulrich of Texas A&M University and colleagues, participants who first viewed a stress-inducing movie, and were then exposed to color/sound videotapes depicting natural scenes, showed much quicker, more complete recovery from stress than those who'd been exposed to videos of urban settings.

These studies and others provide evidence that being in natural spaces— or even just looking out of a window onto a natural scene—somehow soothes us and relieves stress.Gregory Bratman of Stanford University has found evidence that nature may impact our mood in other ways, too.

In one 2015 study, he and his colleagues randomly assigned 60 participants to a 50-minute walk in either a natural setting (oak woodlands) or an urban setting (along a four-lane road). Before and after the walk, the participants were assessed on their emotional state and on cognitive measures, such as how well they could perform tasks requiring short-term memory. Results showed that those who walked in nature experienced less anxiety, rumination (focused attention on negative aspects of oneself), and negative affect, as well as more positive emotions, in comparison to the urban walkers. They also improved their performance on the memory tasks.

Chapter 11:

9 Tips To Reduce Stress

Stress and anxiety are common experiences for most people. In fact, 70% of adults in the United States say they feel stress or anxiety daily. Here are 16 simple ways to relieve stress and anxiety.

1. Exercise

Exercise is one of the most important things you can do to combat stress. It might seem contradictory but putting physical stress on your body through exercise can relieve mental stress. The benefits are strongest when you exercise regularly. People who exercise regularly are less likely to experience anxiety than those who don't exercise. Activities such as walking or jogging that involve repetitive movements of large muscle groups can be particularly stress relieving.

2. Consider Supplements

Several supplements promote stress and anxiety reduction. Here is a brief overview of some of the most common ones:

Lemon balm: Lemon balm is a member of the mint family that has been studied for its anti-anxiety effects.

Omega-3 fatty acids: One study showed that medical students who received omega-3 supplements experienced a 20% reduction in anxiety symptoms.

Ashwagandha: Ashwagandha is an herb used in Ayurvedic medicine to treat stress and anxiety. Several studies suggest that it's effective.

Green tea: Green tea contains many polyphenol antioxidants which provide health benefits. It may lower stress and anxiety by increasing serotonin levels.

Valerian: Valerian root is a popular sleep aid due to its tranquilizing effect. It contains valerenic acid, which alters gamma-aminobutyric acid (GABA) receptors to lower anxiety.

Some supplements can interact with medications or have side effects, so you may want to consult with a doctor if you have a medical condition.

3. Light A Candle

Using essential oils or burning a scented candle may help reduce your feelings of stress and anxiety.

Some scents are especially soothing. Here are some of the most calming scents:

- Lavender
- Rose
- Vetiver
- Bergamot
- Roman chamomile
- Neroli
- Frankincense
- Orange or orange blossom
- Geranium

Using scents to treat your mood is called aromatherapy. Several studies show that aromatherapy can decrease anxiety and improve sleep.

4. Reduce Your Caffeine Intake

Caffeine is a stimulant found in coffee, tea, chocolate and energy drinks. High doses can increase anxiety. People have different thresholds for how much caffeine they can tolerate. If you notice that caffeine makes you jittery or anxious, consider cutting back. Although many studies show that coffee can be healthy in moderation, it's not for everyone. In general, five or fewer cups per day is considered a moderate amount.

5. Write It Down

One way to handle stress is to write things down. While recording what you're stressed about is one approach, another is jotting down what you're grateful for. Gratitude may help relieve stress and anxiety by focusing your thoughts on what's positive in your life.

6. Chew Gum

For a super easy and quick stress reliever, try chewing a stick of gum. One study showed that people who chewed gum had a greater sense of wellbeing and lower stress. One possible explanation is that chewing gum causes brain waves similar to those of relaxed people. Another is that chewing gum promotes blood flow to your brain. Additionally, one recent study found that stress relief was greatest when people chewed more strongly.

7. Spend Time with Friends And Family

Social support from friends and family can help you get through stressful times. Being part of a friend network gives you a sense of belonging and self-worth, which can help you in tough times. One study found that for women in particular, spending time with friends and children helps release oxytocin, a natural stress reliever. This effect is called "tend and befriend," and is the opposite of the fight-or-flight response. Keep in mind that both men and women benefit from friendship. Another study found that men and women with the fewest social connections were more likely to suffer from depression and anxiety.

8. Laugh

It's hard to feel anxious when you're laughing. It's good for your health, and there are a few ways it may help relieve stress: Relieving your stress response. Relieving tension by relaxing your muscles.

In the long term, laughter can also help improve your immune system and mood. A study among people with cancer found that people in the laughter intervention group experienced more stress relief than those who were simply distracted. Try watching a funny TV show or hanging out with friends who make you laugh.

9. Learn To Say No

Try not to take on more than you can handle. Saying no is one way to control your stressors.

Chapter 12:

10 Mental Illness Signs You Should Not Ignore

Can you remember the last time you felt sad, anxious or scared that made you feel different and a little off? The National Alliance of Mental Illness suggests that a rough patch or unusual feelings for a prolonged time can be a sign of something deeper.

There is till stigma around mental illness in our society. The fight against mental illness would become so much easier if we understood its effects and were empathetic.

Here are a few signs and symptoms that can help people recognise their mental health issues or help others.

1. Feeling Sad for Longer Time

Your feelings of sadness that lasts for more than two weeks can be a sign of mental illness. Everyone experiences sadness at one point or the other. However, normal feelings of sadness get better with time. The American Psychiatric Association reported that abnormally intense sadness lasting for two weeks or longer could be a sign of depression. NIH stated that a feeling which is heavier than normal and is difficult to snap out of requires immediate attention.

2. Extreme Mood Swings

You may experience extreme mood swings and may not be able to find a reason behind it. Your mood may seem to switch quickly and randomly. According to a study by National Biotechnology and Information, a person experiences joyous emotions more frequently than the negative ones but it is normal for someone's emotions to change daily. However, according to NAMI, dramatic mood swings that causes shift in behaviour and energy can be a sign of bipolar disorder.

3. Feeling Overanxious

You may feel overanxious at times and feel that you don't have control over your emotions. There might be times when you cannot shut down your mind to keep such thoughts away. According to the National Institute of Mental Health, these may be signs of anxiety disorder. Other signs may include insomnia, irritability, unreasonable aches and pains. If these signs exist for more than six months, one must see a mental health specialist.

4. Isolating Yourself

Other sign may be withdrawal from social activities and isolating oneself. Taking time from others has proven to be beneficial for the physical and mental health of a person. But it is different when you start to make excuses to avoid get-togethers and social interactions often. Avoiding meeting people can be a sign of anxiety or other disorder.

5. Delusions or Hallucinations

According to NAMI, Schizophrenia may be the most poorly understood and stigmatized mental illness diagnosis. It affects less than 1 percent of the population and begins early in life, especially in males. Contrary to inaccurate generalizations, it is possible to live a good life with schizophrenia.

6. Difficulty in Daily Life

People who might be suffering from mental illness may have difficulty in performing their day-to-day tasks and may face problems in daily situations. The Australian Department of Health stated that a rough patch that disrupts your normal functioning and lasts for more than 2 weeks to 2 months may be a sign of depression or anxiety.

7. Sleeping too Much

The Harvard school of Medicine believes that 10-18 percent of people among the normal population face difficulty in sleeping. However, sleeping too much or too little is two or three times more common in people suffering from mental illness like ADHD, depression and anxiety.

8. Drug Abuse

If you might suffer form mental illness you may experience that you have started to abuse alcohol or drugs. According to studies 25 percent of the people who suffer from mental illness resort to alcohol or drugs to curb the feelings of anxiety, anger and mania.

9. Extreme Anger Outbursts

If you ever feel that you can't control your anger or you get angry more frequently than before, it might be a sign of mental illness. The extreme feelings of anger may be warning you about stress, anxiety or the unresolved grief that you might be trying to avoid. Healthline reports suggest that this could be a sign of bipolar disorder, obsessive-compulsive disorder or depression.

10. Thoughts of Self Harm

According to reports by the Mental Health Organization, 10-30 percent of people under the age of 30 have thoughts of self-harm or suicide. The reasons may include neglected or abusive home, loss, or trauma. If you ever find yourself thinking about suicide or self-harm, reach out to a professional for help.

Chapter 13:

7 Tips To Protect Your

Mental Health

We're living in times where everyone is waking up to the daily barrage of upsetting news. From the global pandemic to the enormous omicron wave to the war in Ukraine, there has been a lot going on. It is normal to feel stressed, fearful, anxious, frustrated, lonely, and even angry amid a pandemic, safety, and economic crisis. However, if these issues are not addressed, they can progress into more serious mental health issues that can impact your emotional, psychological, and physical well-being.

Mental health is responsible for your line of thoughts, feelings, and behaviour. Such that, interconnectedness of your thoughts, emotions, or feelings and how you behave says more on how stable your mental health is. In simpler terms, mental health influences how you deal with stress, interacts with others, and make decisions at all stages of your life. It is therefore vital that you learn how to keep your mental state healthy.

Here are 7 tips to protect your mental health.

1. Know That You Are Not Alone

Even up-to date, the topic surrounding mental health is still not openly embraced. People rarely express their feelings and instead try to suppress their negative thoughts and emotions, leading to harmful coping mechanisms. Everyone has had a difficult time in recent years, so know that you are not alone. Seek professional help if necessary, and remember that anxiety and stress are normal and pose no dangers when managed.

2. Wellness Is Being All-Rounded

The principle of well-being is much more than just being physically healthy. It is an integration of your mind and the body with your circumstances. Embracing changes and uncertainties, nurturing your mind and body, building resilience, learning and growing, and doing something meaningful. Although there is no single way of maximizing your mental well-being, self-care practices such as sleep, taking nutritious food, exercise, mindfulness or meditation, or having a "me time" will help protect your mental and physical health

3. Hold Genuine Conversations

Maintaining a healthy and happy mind requires removing yourself from unhealthy or toxic relationships altogether. It also implies keeping close a positive support system instead of withdrawing completely from other people. Isolation is unhealthy, but connecting with people profoundly and honestly is capable of improving your overall well-being. Make a conscious effort to keep in contact with the people who bring you joy.

4. Stop Self-Medicating

If you are someone who goes for hooks such as alcohol, drugs, caffeine, or sweets to feel numb or increase your energy, you are harming your mental health. Don't succumb to the temptation of the "happy hour" as it will only worsen the situation. Excessive consumption of alcohol, caffeine, or drugs has been linked to frequent anxiety attacks. It's time to try your "new go-to" to boost your endorphins and dopamine levels.

5. Step Back and Take Deep Breathes

Several factors influence how healthy you're psychologically and physically. It is very easy to get caught up in making ends meet that you forget to embark on the simple things that protect your well-being. Maintain a meaningful struggle by limiting your focus to one or two things that matter most. Delegate some if need be and direct your energy on doing something good for your well-being.

6. Practice Gratitude

It's imperative to take a moment and appreciate the fact there was a time when you had a great experience. Appreciating the little things allows you to see life in a new light. For example, if you are stressed, focus your attention on the tiny things that once brought you joy. Practicing gratitude allows you to remember all the positive experiences.

7. Be King to Your Sweet Self

Research conducted by psychologist Kristin Neff has demonstrated the importance of treating yourself compassionately in coping with emotional issues and distress. To alleviate these feelings, acknowledge your struggles with kindness rather than beating yourself up or judging yourself. Avoid worsening the situation than it is already.

Conclusion

Whatever is going on with you, keep in mind that your mental health is crucial. Whatever you're dealing with, protecting your mental well-being is critical if you want to be productive and happy. Create some time for yourself and do everything it takes to overcome stress.

Chapter 14:

How To Deal with Feeling Anxious In A Relationship

There are different ways in which relationship anxiety can show up. A lot of people, when they are forming a commitment or when they are in the early stages of their relationship, feel a little insecure now; this is not something we would consider unusual, so if you have doubts or fears, you don't need to worry if they are not affecting you a lot. But sometimes, what happens is that these doubts and anxious thoughts creep into your day-to-day life.

We will list some of the signs of relationship anxiety so you can figure them out for yourself, and then we will tell you how to deal with them.

1. Wondering if you matter to your partner
2. Worrying they want to breakup
3. Doubting your partners feeling for you
4. Sabotaging the relationship

These are some of the signs of relationship anxiety; now, it can take time to get to the roots of what is causing this. Right now, we will tell you how you can overcome it; yes, you read that right, you can overcome it no matter how hard it feels like at the moment. However, it will take time and consistent effort. The first thing you should do is manage anxiety early as soon as you see the symptoms because you keep delaying it. It will become a problem for you. What will help you is maintaining your identity. When you and your partner start getting closer, you will shift the key parts of your identity to make room for your partner and the relationship. You need to know that this does not help either of you. You will lose yourself, and your partner will lose the person they fell in love with. Secondly, practice good communication. If there is something specific, they are doing that is fueling your anxiety, whether it's not making their bed after they wake up or spending a lot of time on their phone, talk to them about it and try to be non-accusatory and respective about also use I statement these can be a huge help during such conversations. If you feel like things are getting out of control and you will not handle them on your own, talk to a therapist that will get you some clarity. Because it's a relationship issue, try talking to a therapist that works with couples because that can be particularly helpful for you, so if you both have any underlying needs, the therapist will be able to communicate that in a better way.

Chapter 15:

The Danger of Dwelling on Things

Do you ever go through a phase where you constantly replay old events in your head or worry and fret about what you could have done differently in a particular situation? Or do you obsessively dwell on past events and keep on repeating a loop of overthinking about your problems? Well, you might think that you're being productive by trying to solve your issues, but in reality, it does more harm than good to you.

There is a specific word for the above situation, and it is "Rumination." Ruminating is the process of dwelling on past events that can't be changed. People who have an anxiety-prone personality are more likely to experience this than others. Some examples include replaying conversations, repeating the past negative experiences in your mind, dwelling on injuries or injustices, and always asking seemingly unanswerable questions of "why me?" In all instances of rumination, the point is that the person gets stuck on a single subject, experience, or emotion.

Yale University conducted research that showed women are more likely to ruminate than men, leading to women having a higher risk of depression. Additionally, the study also focused on the fact that rumination prevents people from acknowledging and dealing with their emotions; they try to understand the situation instead of focusing on the feelings that the situation has caused. The impact of rumination is dangerous and is often underestimated. It is also given the name of "the silent mental health problem." It can play a significant role in anything from obsessive-compulsive disorder (OCD) to eating disorders. According to the World Health Organization (WHO), mental health affects one person in every four during their lifetime and is the leading cause of disability globally. In 2010 alone, they were estimated to have cost $2.5 trillion globally by the World Economic Forum.

Dwelling your past and never escaping the loop will affect you negatively that will eventually eat you alive. Some things might help you to overcome this problem. The first is to self-evaluate and dedicate time to whatever it is that's bothering you. Write all your thoughts down on a piece of paper or the notes app on your phone and set aside some time to think about it. Imagine the worst-case scenario that could happen from your dwelling, and then find a way that how you will deal with it. It will eventually leave you calmer and less anxious because a solution would already be in your hands.

Identify your anxiety triggers and the patterns that eventually lead you to rumination. Once you have identified it, focus on what you would do the next time to avoid making those mistakes again. Talking to a friend would be a good solution too. Write about the things that make you happy and the things you are grateful for. Revisit the list every day and focus on the positives.

It may be easier said than done, but accept that everyone makes mistakes, and it's in the past. You have learned from the situations, and now you have to let go and move on. It may not be easy at first but practice it every day. The more you practice, the easier this process will become, and you will eventually find your peace.

Chapter 16:

Meditate to Rewire Your Brain for Happiness

Suppose you've ever read the book Bridge to Terabithia (or seen the movie). In that case, you are familiar with Terabithia – an imaginary world that the main characters, Jesse and Leslie, create as a haven. It is somewhere they can go to be free from the cares and worries of the world.

Meditation has given me a Terabithia. I have created a clearing of calm and tranquility that I can enter into within seconds whenever I feel the need. I have a refuge no matter where I am or what I am doing. The worries of the world no longer threaten me. Except this mental place isn't imaginary, and it isn't populated with trolls and wild creatures – it is as real as the world we live in.

Since starting my meditation habit, my brain has been rewired for happiness, peace, and success. Here are just a few of the benefits:

I rarely become angry.

I find happiness in unexpected places.

I form deeper relationships and build friendships more easily.

However, by far, the largest benefit is that a deep, serene calm and peace is slowly permeating into every area of my life. At first, meditating felt unusual – like I was stepping out of normal life and doing something that most people find strange. I soon realized, however, that this wasn't true – millions of people meditate, and many successful people attribute part of their success to meditation.

Oprah Winfrey, Hugh Jackman, Richard Branson, Paul McCartney, Angelina Jolie… Any of these names sound familiar? All of these are famous meditators.

This list alone is powerful, but maybe you need a little more convincing that meditation is something you should try.

Michael Jordan, Kobe Bryant, Misty-May Trainor, and Derek Jeter are just a few successful athletes who rely on meditation to get them in the zone.

Rupert Murdoch, Russell Simons, and Arianna Huffington all practice meditation.

Arnold Schwarzenegger and Eva Mendez are just a couple more celebrities that make meditation a daily habit.

Meditation Reduces Stress

Are you feeling the weight of the world on your shoulders? Meditation is incredibly effective at reducing stress and anxiety. One study found that mindfulness and Zen-type meditations significantly reduce stress when practiced over a period of three months. Another study revealed that meditation reduces the density of brain tissue associated with anxiety and worrying. If you want your stress levels to plummet, meditation may be the answer.

Chapter 17:

How To Fight Worrying

The Good News

The good news in town is that you should stop worrying. Worry is a feeling of anxiety that stems from fear of failure. Our success is contributed by some factors that we may not have control over. It is unfair for us to judge ourselves harshly based on them.

Worrying will not change anything. We should focus on how we can change the situation instead of worrying about it. We try to meet the expectations that people have of us. The fear of letting them down is a cause of worry.

The Genesis Of Worrying

Worrying is caused by many other factors apart from the expectations of other people on us. We are afraid of letting ourselves down. Our history of failure could haunt us and we become uncertain whether we can change it.

Another cause of worry is the fear of the consequences of non-performance. We are afraid of what may befall us when we fail to succeed.

The genesis of constant worry could also come from childhood trauma. Experiences as children shape our adulthood. There could be no valid reason for us to worry but past experiences can make us always anxious. All reasons for worrying are valid. It is a natural human feeling but we should not allow it to overtake our mental stability.

Stop Worrying

There could be many reasons why you should worry but there are twice as much why you should not. Although worrying is a subconscious emotion that we hardly have control over, we can address the potential sources of worry.

Here is how to:

1. Do Not Be A People-Pleaser

You cannot stop people from having expectations from you on anything. They can have their opinion about your ability and there is nothing you can do about it. However, do not live trying to impress them. You owe them nothing.

Continue pursuing your dreams without gauging yourself against their expectations. You will not strain and wear yourself out as you seek their approval. Prioritize your ambitions above their expectations and you will have nothing to worry about.

2. Be Self-Confident

Believe in yourself even when others doubt you. You will not worry about failure when you are self-confident. The greatest gift to yourself is trusting in your ability to deliver on your mandate. Do not worry about what you cannot control.

Worrying will pressure you to act wrongly. Delayed right action is better than a fast wrong move. Have the mental strength to withstand external pressure and believe in yourself.

3. Face Your Fears

Past trauma could indeed have a long-lasting impact on our adulthood. Our worry could be because of childhood abuse. We were punished when we could not perform and consequently developed performance anxiety.

Stop worrying because that ugly phase has passed. Fight performance anxiety by doing your best. Repeat what you were unable to do in childhood and succeed. You will no longer worry about it in the future.

4. Make A Move

If you can change something, why worry? Still, why worry if you cannot change it? This is a call to action. Worrying alone will change nothing. Do not despise your position. Make a bold move that you see can make things better.

Responsible adulting is proactive. Act without waiting on instructions. Your actions are for the greater good. There could be other people who have the same worry as you. It is a blessing when you make a move and assure them not to worry.

5. Look At The Brighter Side

Learn to look at the good side in every situation. There could be a reason why things are not moving as you expect. Your worry could be a deliberate act of nature for the greater good.

Looking at the brighter side will make you not worry about a lot of things. In due time, everything will work out as planned.

In conclusion, fighting worry is a deliberate decision that we make. Except we do it, no one will do it for you. These five ways will lead you out of worry.

Chapter 18:

How Going Outside More Can Make You Happy

Do you ever find yourself feeling calmer, more relaxed, or more focused after spending time in nature? That's because time outside has studied and proven benefits for your mental health. Mental illness affects one in five humans in any given year. Let's talk about what some Vitamin N (nature) can do for your mental health...

A simple stay in the outdoors can do wonders for relieving anxiety, stress, and depression. Countless studies have proven that nature has a positive effect on your mental health. What you see, hear, and experience in nature can improve your mood in a moment.

There is a strong connection between time spent in nature and reduced negative emotions. This includes symptoms of anxiety, depression, and psychosomatic illnesses like irritability, insomnia, tension headaches, and indigestion. Feeling stressed? Research shows a link between exposure to nature and stress reduction. Stress is relieved within minutes of exposure to nature as measured by muscle tension, blood pressure, and brain activity. Time in green spaces significantly reduces your cortisol, which is a stress hormone. Nature also boosts endorphin levels and dopamine production, which promotes happiness.

Nature has a myriad of other brain benefits as well. Contact with nature has restorative properties, increasing energy and improving feelings of vitality and focus. Being nearby to nature has been shown to reduce symptoms of ADHD. Are you stuck on a project or idea? Being outside also improves creative thinking. Proximity to green space can restore capacity for concentration and attention.

Trouble sleeping? A two-hour walk in the woods is enough to improve sleep quality and help relieve sleep problems. Sleeping away from artificial light and waking up with natural sunlight can reset your circadian rhythm, which will help you feel refreshed after a better night's sleep.

Nature can also help with the grief process. This is because exposure to nature causes better coping, including improved self-awareness, self-concept, and positively affected mood. The positive effects of nature affect the way you treat others. People are more caring and positive when they are exposed to and around various forms of nature.

Getting outdoors doesn't have to be a lot of work. There are lots of simple ways you can get quality time in nature. Start with taking a walk in the woods. Nature walks help combat stress while improving mental well-being. Want to take your walk to the next level? Try forest bathing.

Move your workout into the outdoors. Regular use of natural areas for physical activity can reduce the risk of mental health problems by 50%. Completing activities like walking, cycling, jogging, or doing yoga in a natural environment makes you happier than in the city

Engage your senses to maximize the health benefits of being outside. Breathe deep, as the scent of fresh pine has been shown to lower stress and anxiety. Make sure to pause and listen, as studies show that listening to nature sounds like bird songs and rushing water can help lower stress levels. Book a camping trip. Immersing yourself in nature for a longer period of time is the best way to absorb the health benefits of the outdoors.

Chapter 19:

Living in the Moment

Today we're going to talk about a topic that will help those of you struggling with fears and anxieties about your past and even about your future. And I hope that at the end of this video, you may be able to live a life that is truly more present and full.

So, what is living in the moment all about and why should we even bother?

You see, for many of us, since we're young, we've been told to plan for our future. And we always feel like we're never enough until we achieve the next best grade in class, get into a great university, get a high paying career, and then retire comfortably. We always look at our life as an endless competition, and that we believe that there will always be more time to have fun and enjoy life later when we have worked our asses off and clawed our way to success. Measures that are either set by our parents, society, or our peers. And this constant desire to look ahead, while is a good motivator if done in moderation and not obsessively, can lead us to always being unhappy in our current present moment.

Because we are always chasing something bigger, the goal post keeps moving farther and farther away every time we reach one. And the reality is that we will never ever be happy with ourselves at any point if that becomes our motto. We try to look so far ahead all the time that we miss the beautiful sights along the way. We miss the whole point of our goals which is not to want the end goal so eagerly, but to actually enjoy the process, enjoy the journey, and enjoy each step along the way. The struggles, the sadness, the accomplishments, the joy. When we stop checking out the flowers around us, and when we stop looking around the beautiful sights, the destination becomes less amazing.

Reminding ourselves to live in the present helps us keep things in perspective that yes, even though our ultimate dream is to be this and that career wise, or whatever it may be, that we must not forget that life is precious, and that each day is a blessing and that we should cherish each living day as if it were your last.

Forget the idea that you might have 30 years to work before you can tell ur self that you can finally relax and retire. Because you never know if you will even have tomorrow. If you are always reminded that life is fragile and that your life isn't always guaranteed, that you become more aware that you need to live in the moment in order to live your best life. Rid yourself of any worries, anxieties, and fears you have about the future because the time will come when it comes. Things will happen for you eventually so long as you do what you need to do each and every day without obsessing over it.

Sometimes our past failures and shortcomings in the workplace can have an adverse effect on how we view the present as well. And this cycle perpetuates itself over and over again and we lose sight of what's really important to us. Our family, our friends, our pets, and we neglect them or neglect to spend enough time with them thinking we have so much time left. But we fail to remember again that life does not always work the way we want it to. And we need to be careful not to fall into that trap that we have complete and total control over our life and how our plans would work out.

In the next video we will talk about how to live in the moment if you have anxieties and fears about things unrelated to work. Whether it be a family issue or a health issue. I want to address that in a separate topic.

Chapter 20:

Stop Dwelling on Things

It's 5 p.m., the deadline for an important work project is at 6, and all you can think about is the fight you had with the next-door neighbor this morning. You're dwelling. "It's natural to look inward," but while most people pull out when they've done it enough, an overthinker will stay in the loop."

Ruminating regularly often leads to depression. So, if you're prone to obsessing (and you know who you are), try these tactics to head off the next full-tilt mental spin cycle...

1.Distract Yourself

Go and exercise, scrub the bathtub spotless, put on music and dance, do whatever engrosses you, and do it for at least 10 minutes. That's the minimum time required to break a cycle of thoughts.

2. Make a Date to Dwell

Tell yourself you can obsess all you want from 6 to 7 p.m., but until then, you're banned. "By 6 p.m., you'll probably be able to think things through more clearly,"

3. 3 Minutes of Mindfulness

For one minute, eyes closed, acknowledge all the thoughts going through your mind. For the next minute, just focus on your breathing. Spend the last minute expanding your awareness from your breath to your entire body. "Paying attention in this way gives you the room to see the questions you're asking yourself with less urgency and to reconsider them from a different perspective,"

4.The Best and Worst Scenarios

Ask yourself...

"What's the worst that could happen?" and "How would I cope?" Visualizing yourself handling the most extreme outcome should alleviate some anxiety. Then consider the likelihood that the worst will occur.

Next, imagine the best possible outcome; by this point, you'll be in a more positive frame of mind and better able to assess the situation more realistically.

5. Call a Friend

Ask a friend or relative to be your point person when your thoughts start to speed out of control.

6. Is It Worth It?

If you find that your mind is fixated on a certain situation, ask yourself if the dwelling is worth your time.

'Ask yourself if looking over a certain situation will help you accept it, learn from it and find closure,' 'If the answer is no, you should make a conscious effort to shelve the issue and move on from it.'

7. Identify Your Anxiety Trigger

There may be a pattern in your worries, and this means you can help identify potential causes and use practice preventative measures.

'For many of us, rumination will occur after a trigger, so it is important to identify what it is,' 'For example, if you have to give a presentation at work and the last one you didn't go to plan, this can cause rumination and anxiety.

Chapter 21:

How Volunteering Can Make You Happy

With busy lives, it can be hard to find time to volunteer. However, the benefits of volunteering can be enormous. Volunteering offers vital help to people in need, worthwhile causes, and the community, but the benefits can be even greater for you, the volunteer. The right match can help you to find friends, connect with the community, learn new skills, and even advance your career.

Giving to others can also help protect your mental and physical health. It can reduce stress, combat depression, keep you mentally stimulated, and provide a sense of purpose. While it's true that the more you volunteer, the more benefits you'll experience, volunteering doesn't have to involve a long-term commitment or take a huge amount of time out of your busy day. Giving in even simple ways can help those in need and improve your health and happiness.

One of the more well-known benefits of volunteering is the impact on the community. Volunteering allows you to connect to your community and make it a better place. Even helping out with the smallest tasks can make a real difference to the lives of people, animals, and organizations in need. And volunteering is a two-way street: It can benefit you and your family as much as the cause you choose to help. Dedicating your time as a volunteer helps you make new friends, expand your network, and boost your social skills.

One of the best ways to make new friends and strengthen existing relationships is to commit to a shared activity together. Volunteering is a great way to meet new people, especially if you are new to an area. It strengthens your ties to the community and broadens your support network, exposing you to people with common interests, neighbourhood resources, and fun and fulfilling activities.

While some people are naturally outgoing, others are shy and have a hard time meeting new people. Volunteering gives you the opportunity to practice and develop your social skills, since you are meeting regularly with a group of people with common interests. Once you have momentum, it's easier to branch out and make more friends and contacts. Volunteering helps counteract the effects of stress, anger, and anxiety; The social contact aspect of helping and working with others can have a profound effect on your overall psychological well-being.

Nothing relieves stress better than a meaningful connection to another person. Working with pets and other animals has also been shown to improve mood and reduce stress and anxiety.
Volunteering combats depression; Volunteering keeps you in regular contact with others and helps you develop a solid support system, which in turn protects you against depression.

Volunteering makes you happy; By measuring hormones and brain activity, researchers have discovered that being helpful to others delivers immense pleasure. Human beings are hard-wired to give to others. The more we give, the happier we feel.

Chapter 22:

Feeling like You're Drowning in Stuff

By drowning, the first thing that comes to mind is drowning in A pool of water. Well, drowning in life is almost the same as drowning in water. Every time you drown, you need the help of A lifeguard or any other guy who can drag you out and save you. The same is the case with drowning in life; if you don't dig deep enough to come out of this phase, you need the help of an expert to help you feel better. When A person feels like drowning in stuff, most of the time, the reason is the hectic daily routine or the rush of emotions. When emotions start to build up to an extent where they become A burden, the affected person feels like being drowned in these emotions. This can further lead to stress and anxiety. If the feeling is due to work, it's because the person is working more than his brain and body can handle. This mostly happens to students who are working part-time to manage their expenses. The burden of study is already A big one, and once coupled to the workload, it becomes A mountain of A burden where the student doesn't get any time to relax.

There are many ways to overcome this feeling. The most effective one is to let your emotions out. Some councilors are there to listen to one's problems and find the perfect solution to them. If A person chooses to remain silent, he will be overwhelmed by these emotions/thoughts, and that is when these feelings turn into depression and anxiety. When depression kicks in, it's even harder to get back on track than it is when you are starting to have feelings of drowning. Now for students who are also working, they should find A way to relax every now and then. Relaxation is always A good solution to these problems. Taking some time out for yourself can prove to be healthy for both the body and the brain. The mind always produces positive thoughts when it is relaxed. Overburdening can lead to negative emotions and thoughts, which can lead to the feeling of being drowned.

Working out can be very helpful in times like these. It releases A hormone called endorphin which actually helps with stress and gives you joyful emotions. When the body is engaged in repetitive motions, the brain gets distracted from all burdens and only focuses on the tasks at hand, which in this case is exercise. So focusing only on one task helps the brain to relax and heal from all of the thoughts that were being processed before. After the workout, the person feels very light and positive because of this short relaxation of the brain.

Mental health professionals are there for those who are having A hard time dealing with the feeling of being drowned in stuff. One should never feel ashamed of talking to somebody about matters like these because it is for their good. Relying on medicines and other relaxants can lead to improper functioning of the brain. Still, practicing habits like taking counsel from professionals or simply giving time to oneself can prove to be very healthy as it helps the mind to focus better. Giving up isn't the option; surviving and eventually living the best life is.

Chapter 23:

Five Ways To Get Calm

The art of maintaining calm.

Calmness is an art that only a few people have mastered. Most people are erratic and easily unsettled by trivial matters. The state of calmness provides an optimum environment to work and meet your targets.

The modern world is full of people who seek solace in different deviations. They hope to find peace in a chaotic world. However, they only find temporary solutions to their problems and fail to secure calmness of mind and spirit.

Here are five ways to get calm:

1. Regulate Your Body's Metabolism

We may find ourselves in circumstances that make our bodies tense. We experience an adrenaline rush as a natural body response to tension. Our hearts beat faster, a pang of fear laced with anxiety sweeps through our minds, and we are unable to make sober decisions.

Calmness becomes elusive and we often act out of fear of the unknown. In such circumstances, our actions are not backed up by any rational thinking. How can we regain our composure and maintain calm? First, inhale sharply and exhale slowly to release the tension building up.

Repeat it until you manage to regulate your breathing. Inhaling and exhaling at regular intervals will bring calmness to replace the initial tension. Try to act as normal as possible and do not yield to any pressure to act, real or perceived.

2. Master Your Emotions

It takes great courage to master your emotions and reactions towards issues. A great man is capable of controlling his emotions and bringing calmness in chaotic situations. Calmness hardly prevails when emotions are high.

Emotions rid you of rationality and independent thinking. They control your actions and seek justification. Emotions are no respecter of persons. They have caused the downfall of many giants who did not let reason prevail.

Take charge of your emotions and do not yield to their temptations no matter how justifiable they may look. A master of emotions will bring calmness in their lives and they can settle things soberly.

3. Question Your Feelings

Your feelings are not always right. You could be biased and inclined to support certain things that disrupt calmness and are fodder to chaos. Subconscious feelings often present themselves as the truth and we believe unfounded theories that pose a danger to interpersonal relationships and by extension, societal harmony.

Calmness prevails where feelings and intuitions are evaluated before being acted upon. Learn to question your feelings and leave nothing to chance. For example, why do you hate the guard at the main gate or a political competitor? It is unfair to yourself not to understand the reason for the strong positions you take.

After questioning your feelings, you can re-evaluate hardline stances that you took which can jeopardize your calmness around people you consider hostile. You can manage to be calm and tolerant when you find no merit in your ill feelings towards something.

4. Question What You Stand to Benefit Or Lose

The chief question you should be able to answer is what you benefit from any chaos. There is disorderliness in the absence of calm, and it causes more harm than good. We are exposed to the risk of loss when the environment we live in is unstable. It is important to ensure it is calm for us to thrive in it and achieve our goals.

Many things run in the mind when one is provoked. What often skips the brain is whether or not the whole experience will be gainful. At this juncture, you think in retrospect concerning your life. Will a moment of anger make you lose what has taken long for you to build?

Such hard questions will eventually let calmness prevail. The fear of losing precious gains will bring calmness to maintain the status quo.

5. Selective Amnesia

Amnesia is a condition of forgetting things. The memory is compromised and one forgets everything that happened in their lives. It is undesirable but maybe you should consider it if you want to be calm. Selective amnesia is choosing to willfully ignore the ugly things that have happened.

When you realize that something irritates you, shut it out of your life to regain sanity. Calmness is an expensive gift that should be treasured. Nothing should deprive you of the right to enjoy the serenity of life.

Choose to look at the good side only of things. You can maintain calm by dwelling exclusively on it and refusing to give people the power to control you.

In conclusion, calmness is a trophy that should be on our shelves. These five ways to get calm are effective should we implement them correctly.

Chapter 24:

3 Ways To Calm The Emotional Storm Within You

When emotions are already intense, it's often hard to think about what you can do to help yourself, so the first thing you need to work on is getting re-regulated as quickly as possible. Here are some fast-acting skills that work by changing your body's chemistry; it will be most helpful if you first try these before you're in an emotional situation, so you know how to use them.

1. Do A Forward Bend

This is my favorite re-regulating skill. Bend over as though you're trying to touch your toes (it doesn't matter if you can actually touch your toes; you can also do this sitting down if you need to, by sticking your head between your knees). Take some slow, deep breaths, and hang out there for a little while (30 to 60 seconds if you can). Doing a forward bend actually activates our parasympathetic nervous system – our 'rest and digest' system – which helps us slow down and feel a little calmer. When you're ready to stand up again, just don't do it too quickly – you don't want to fall over.

2. Focus On Your Exhale With 'Paced Breathing'

It might sound like a cliché but breathing truly is one of the best ways to get your emotions to a more manageable level. In particular, focus on making your exhale longer than your inhale – this also activates our parasympathetic nervous system, again helping us feel a little calmer and getting those emotions back to a more manageable level. When you inhale, count in your head to see how long your inhale is; as you exhale, count at the same pace, ensuring your exhale is at least a little bit longer than your inhale. For example, if you get to 4 when you inhale, make sure you exhale to at least 5. For a double whammy, do this breathing while doing your forward bend.

These re-regulating skills will help you to think a little more clearly for a few minutes, but your emotions will start to intensify once more if nothing else has changed in your environment – so the next steps are needed too.

3. Increase Awareness Of Your Emotions

In order to manage emotions more effectively in the long run, you need to be more aware of your emotions and of all their components; and you need to learn to name your emotions accurately. This might sound strange – of course you know what you're feeling, right? But how do you know if what you've always called 'anger' is actually anger, and not anxiety? Most of us have never really given our emotions much thought, we just assume that what we think we feel is what we actually feel – just like we assume the colour we've always called 'blue' is actually blue; but how do we really know?

Sensitive people who have grown up in a pervasively invalidating environment often learn to ignore or not trust their emotional experiences, and try to avoid or escape those experiences, which contributes to difficulties naming emotions accurately. Indeed, anyone prone to emotion dysregulation can have trouble figuring out what they're feeling, and so walks around in an emotional 'fog'. When you're feeling 'upset', 'bad' or 'off', are you able to identify what emotion you're actually feeling? If you struggle with this, consider each of the following questions the next time you experience even a mild emotion:

- What was the prompting event or trigger for the feeling? What were you reacting to? (Don't judge whether your response was right or wrong, just be descriptive.)

- What were your thoughts about the situation? How did you interpret what was happening? Did you notice yourself judging, jumping to conclusions, or making assumptions?

- What did you notice in your body? For example, tension or tightness in certain areas? Changes in your breathing, your heart rate, your temperature?

- What was your body doing? Describe your body language, posture and facial expression.

- What urges were you noticing? Did you want to yell or throw things? Was the urge to not make eye contact, to avoid or escape a situation you were in?

- What were your actions? Did you act on any of the urges you noted above? Did you do something else instead?

Going through this exercise will help you increase your ability to name your emotions accurately. Once you've asked yourself the above questions, you could try asking yourself if your emotion fits into one of these four (almost rhyming) categories: mad, sad, glad, and afraid. These are terms I use with clients as a helpful starting point for distinguishing basic emotions, but gradually you can work on getting more specific; emotions lists can also be helpful.

Chapter 25:

4 Reasons Why You Feel Empty

The feeling of emptiness is stark in contrast to the emotions that a person is supposed to feel. It sits like a black hole in your chest, devoid of the substance that is supposed to be there. Here are some of the reasons why you feel empty

1. Absence Of Purpose

Many people struggle with finding a sense of purpose in this vast universe of limitless possibilities.

What do I do with my life? Does this mean anything? What should I be doing with myself?

The existential dread that comes with lacking purpose can fuel emptiness as it feels like we are missing something we are supposed to have. Some people try to fill the emptiness with their actions, like doing volunteer work or getting a job in a field that can help people.

Seeking purpose is an interesting matter because you may not be ready to find a particular purpose. And we don't mean that in an abstract, destiny kind of sense. Instead, there might be life experiences you need to have and work you need to do before a fulfilling purpose can click with you.

Perhaps being a parent offers you the kind of fulfillment that would fill that emptiness, but you wouldn't necessarily know that until after you have a child. Or maybe it's something more career-focused. Maybe your heart and mind are in tune with being on the sea, something you may not know until you set foot on a boat.

You may even feel a pull toward something that could offer you fulfillment, like a persistent interest or something that really speaks to you. That could help you find a direction.

2. Grief, The Death Of A Loved One

Grief is a natural emotional reaction to the death of a loved one. Sometimes we can see the end coming and have some time to mentally and emotionally prepare for it. Other times we may lose a loved one unexpectedly. There is always a flood of emotions to deal with when a death occurs, even if it's not immediate.

Many people turn to grief models to better try to process and understand their grief without really understanding the models. The "Five Stages of Grief" is one such model. What people tend to get wrong about these models is that they are not hard and fast rules. It's impossible to shove the full scope of emotions into such a narrow box, a fact that the creators of such models regularly talk about.

They may serve as a general guideline. There are stages that you may or may not experience. Some people experience multiple stages at the same time. Others bounce around through different stages as they are mourning their loved one.

Many of the models talk about "numbness" or "denial" as being involved in the grief process and this might explain the emptiness you feel. It can be a difficult experience because, rationally, you know that you should probably be feeling sadness along with lots of other emotions, but you don't and that's hard to reconcile.

Grief and mourning are more complicated than they appear. That makes it a good idea to seek a grief counselor. A grief specialist may be able to help you through those persistent empty feelings and mourning.

3. Drug And Alcohol Abuse

Many people turn to drugs and alcohol to cope with the traumas of their life. There's nothing inherently wrong with periodically having a drink or using legal substances. The problems really start to pick up when those substances are used excessively or as a way to help moderate one's emotions.

Filling the void of emptiness with a substance can lead to addiction, worse relationships with other people, losing jobs, and changing life circumstances.

Substance abuse can also lead to different physical or mental health issues, other than substance abuse disorder, like sparking a latent mental illness or liver disease. It may also make preexisting health issues worse.

Alcohol is known to impact people with mood disorders, like depression and bipolar disorder, far more severely than people without. It just works differently in their minds and may fuel emotional instability and make depression worse.

One of the reasons people use substances is to help them survive something they are going through. They believe it helps them because it calms them down at the moment. The problem is that extended substance use can have long-term effects that can worsen mental health issues or cause new ones to crop up in the future.

4. Long-Term Stresses

Humans aren't built to cope with long-term stresses well. Stress causes different hormones to be produced to help a person get through that immediate stressful situation, but those hormones can cause more significant problems the longer they are present.

Long-term stresses can cause depression, anxiety, and in some cases, PTSD. Survivors of domestic abuse, child abuse, and poverty may develop Complex PTSD, which results from never really getting a break from the circumstances they survived.

Avoiding long-term stresses or changing living situations may help. But if mental health problems have developed, it will require a trained mental health professional to heal and recover from.

Chapter 26:

Stop Giving a Damn About Everything

Our life is a series of decisions and the consequences of those decisions. But these decisions are not wholly of ours. They have been approved by many people, society, friends, family, and even the people we don't know. We care more about what people think about us than what makes us happy, and we are habitual of taking consent from others.

Have you ever thought about what privileges does it give you? Nothing! Except killing your self-esteem and making you insecure in public. Others grade our daily day-to-day choices to our career and job decisions.

You managed to impress them, but what good does it bring to you?

It all leads to stress and anxiety stealing away your peace and leaving you in a constant struggle between your happiness and seeking approval.

Life settlements should be based on your desires and your definition of contentment. After all, it's your life, and you be the one living with the consequences.

You choose a job or a lifestyle that isn't what you craved for, and it's what your family wanted for you. And you are stuck with a 9 to 5 job you never wanted, and you are giving your hours and energy without an ounce of satisfaction.

You can't control everything in your life, but you can choose how to react to it. Everything that happens around you is not your headache, and what people might say about you is not something you should be bothered by.

Just like your business is not someone else's business, their business is not your business. The rule to a peaceful life is
"Mind your own business."
Someone bought a sports car, got fired, looked prettier than you, or was smiling all day. It would help if you were least concerned about all this. Nagging about someone's personal affairs might not affect them much, but it surely will destroy your tranquility.
Learn to be content in every situation. Develop an attitude of caring less.
Is someone better than you? So what?
Did someone leave you? What's the big deal?

By acknowledging priorities in your life, you can stop giving a damn to people and everything. You can't just care about anything, and there has to be something specific. Align your ambitions and passions. Set your goals and fight your way towards them. You are going to meet a lot of people on your road who won't agree with you, but you are not here to impress them.

A happy person will criticize others less and will show more empathy. What someone opinions about you is his mindset. If you start listening to everyone on your road, do you think you'll ever make it to the end.? If you are going to stop and heed them? Then what about your motives and targets? Elements that you should be working on will lay neglected.

You have to be passionate about something in your life, a weighted purpose to stop caring about worthless things. And strive for it. Keeping your body and mind busy for a more significant cause makes you unaware of all the trivial matters.

As you progress in life, priorities tend to shift. You should know what holds the highest value and focus on those points that eventually lead to your happiness, give yourself more credit and appropriate your flaws.

Chapter 27:

Stop Overthinking

Thinking Optimally

Thinking is healthy for everybody. The fact that you do not think about anything is a red flag. Thinking gives you a range of choices in decision-making. You can evaluate one after another before settling for the best.

Good thinking is not a choice we have anyway. If you do not do it, somebody else will exploit you by thinking on your behalf. They may not act in good faith and you will be the victim.

Thinking is healthy and normal for any sane person. However, there are upper and lower limits in thinking. Retarded thinking will disable you from living or working optimally. Similarly, overthinking will deny you serenity in life.

Threshold Of Thoughts To Entertain

We should not every thought regardless of how enticing they are because their effects could be disastrous. We should sieve whatever we give attention to while allowing only the best to occupy our minds. However, do we have control over our thoughts?

Most people cannot take charge of their thoughts because they have not set their priorities right. Their minds cannot prioritize what is important because of their indecisiveness. They cannot let go of an idea or situation once they start pondering on it.

Overthinking is highly unrecompensed. Here are a few ways on how to stop it:

1. Accept Fate

Fate is unchallengeable. There is a different way to handle it if it is unfavorable. Living in denial will complicate matters instead of making them better. Be optimistic when doors shut in front of you. Consider it a way nature is warning you about the path you have chosen.

The universe naturally selects the best for us. Its blessings could come in unexpected ways. When we misjudge them for misfortunes, we will spend much time overthinking what we should have thanked the universe for.

Accepting fate is not giving up. It is stopping to overthink non-issues and moving on to more important ones. Overthinking is injurious to an uncertain future. We can bulldoze our way in things that we could have just left alone. Such mistakes are expensive to commit.

2. Count Your Blessings

One reason why people overthink is the fear of losing. It clouds their judgment to the extent of not remembering their past achievements. Think enough to get past a hurdle but do not prolong it further. Overthinking will not make problems go away. Instead, it could complicate them more.

Whenever you find yourself overthinking about something, retract your steps and be grateful for your achievements. Gratitude will open your eyes to the reality that you did not make it because of overthinking. Other factors were part of your success.

Overthinking will blind you from acknowledging your past victories. Fight it by reminding yourself that it had nothing to do with your success.

3. Prioritize Your Health

A healthy lifestyle is worry-free. You can stop overthinking when you consider the status of your health. It does more harm than good. People with underlying health conditions like high blood pressure and diabetes are advised by doctors not to overthink for the sake of their health.

Overthinking could trigger ulcers. For the sake of good health, strive not to overthink trivial issues. Whenever you start overthinking, remember what it can do to your health. Prioritize your health above everything.

Consider the analogy of cigarette smokers and the health warning written boldly on the packets. If they could take the warning seriously, a majority of them would not fall to lung-related complications in old age. Similarly, there is a warning to stop overthinking in life lest you succumb to depression and anxiety.

In conclusion, it is paramount to stop overthinking because it changes nothing. Its demerits outweigh its benefits. It is a passive way of dealing with challenges. Instead of worrying about a problem, be proactive in seeking solutions.

When the burden of overthinking gets heavy, share it with your friends and you will find a solution together.

Chapter 28:

Meditate For Focus

Meditation calms the mind and helps you to focus on what is important. It dims the noise and brings your goals into clearer vision.

Meditation has been practiced as far back as 5000bc in India - with meditation depicted in wall artisan from that period.

That is 1500 years older than any written artefact ever found.

It is as old as the archaeological evidence of any human society.

Meditation can change the structure of the brain promoting focus, learning and better memory, as well as lowering stress and reducing the chances of anxiety and depression.

Whilst there are many different types and ways to meditate,

the ultimate goal is to clear your mind and calm your body

so that you can focus on your dream.

Aim to look inward for answers.

It could be aided by music relating to your dream or videos.

The music, the images, and imagining you are already living that life will bring it into reality.

Your mind creates the vision and the feeling
in your heart will bring it to you.
When your mind and heart work together it creates balance,
leading to happiness and success.

Meditation is the process of bringing the
visions of the mind and the desires of the heart together,
which in turn will form your life.
Meditation clears all the threats to this -
such as worry and distraction.
It will bring you clear focus and open up the next steps in your journey.

Meditation is often best done when you first wake or before you go to
sleep, but it can be incorporated into your day.
If clear consistent thought brings decisive action and success,
it is important to dwell on your dreams as often as possible.
Calm your mind of the unnecessary noise that is robbing you of your
focus.

The more realistic you make this vision
and the more you feel it in your heart,
the quicker it will come.

Meditation can help you achieve this
whether you follow a guide or make it up yourself.
The key is calm and focus.

Your subconscious knows how to get there.

Meditation will help open up that knowledge.

Science is just beginning to unlock the answers on why meditation is so effective, even so it has been used for over 7000 years to help people relax and focus on their goals.

The positive health and well-being evidence of meditation is well documented.

We may not yet understand it fully,

But just know that it works and use it every day.

You don't need to understand every detail to use something that works.

Meditation is perhaps one of the most time-tested tools in existence.

It could work for you, if you try it.

It could change your life forever.

Chapter 29:

Meditation The Key To Happiness

Have you ever wondered why people who meditate tend to be the happiest, most grateful and satisfied people on earth? And have you ever wondered why the rest of us always seem to be unhappy about everything that is going on with our lives even though we are incredibly fortunate to be alive?

Many of us have a roof over our heads, smartphones that keeps us connected all the time, friends and family that surround us, but yet we still can't explain why we aren't at peace inside.

We get bogged down by traffic, people around us who seem to rub us the wrong way, and the countless other things that seem to bring us closer and closer to anguish.

Another problem that many of us have to deal with right now is stress. we have deadlines, colleagues, bosses, and paperwork that bring us overwhelm on a daily basis that we find ourselves off balance and in search of our breath.

I want to introduce you to the powerful tool called meditation, and why it is crucial that you employ it in your lives to reduce stress and anxiety and to live a more mindful life starting today.

When we meditate, even to a short 5-10min guided meditation practice that can be found on YouTube or even right here on this channel, we bring our awareness to the present moment. And when we breathe and focus on the breath, we allow time for ourselves to be grounded and centered. When thoughts enter our mind, we simply acknowledge them and let them drift on by. This conscious practice of being fully present and deep breathing allows our bodies to relax and destress. And we are much more focused on what we need to do and how we can get to our goals faster.

Through meditation, one can change and rewire our brain to stop thinking of the past and future but to focus on the here and now. With intention, meditation can also help you get what you needed to done faster.

Through my own meditation practice, I have found that it made every day of my life much more purposeful and grounded. Before, i always found myself drifting throughout the day, wasting time, procrastinating, and feeling guilty for not taking action. But with a simple 10min guided meditation practice, I was able to refocus my attention and get my day going as it should without feeling sorry that I had wasted my morning not getting anything done.

Meditation takes time to develop, like a muscle, consistency is the key to success. By devoting 10mins each day to meditation, you are telling yourself that this is the time for yourself, time to reframe all the negative thoughts, to be grateful for your existence, to not dwell on the past, and to focus on the things and people that matter in life. Your body will essentially be "tricked" into automatically feeling abundance, happiness, and joy. The more you do it, the more powerful this technique becomes.

I challenge each and every one of you to try out meditation for yourself, even if i am only able to get through to one person, I am sure you will experience the rich and rewarding experience that meditation can do for you today.

Chapter 30:

The Power of Breathing To Reset Your Mind

Breathing is something we often take for granted. The breath is always there where we notice or not, keeping us going, and keeping us alive. Without our breath, our hearts will not have enough oxygen and we will die a very agonizing death. Yet many of us forget to take the time out of the day to utilize this powerful tool of breathing mindfully to reset our focus, and to calm ourselves down in times of stress and anxiety.

Throughout the way, we are bombarded with things. Work stuff, people stuff, family stuff, and our minds and hearts begin racing and stay elevated throughout the day. Induced by stress hormones, we find ourselves full of cluttered thoughts and our productivity and focus drops as a result. Without clearing all these negative emotions that are bottled up inside us, we may find ourselves stressed out and unable to relax throughout the day, and even at night as we try to go to sleep.

This is where the power of conscious breathing comes into play. We all have the power and choice to take 30 seconds out of our day each time we feel that we need to settle down our emotions and clear our head.

Everytime you feel like things are getting out of control, simply stop whatever you are doing, close your eyes, and focus on breathing through our noise. Notice the breath that goes in and out of your nostrils as you inhale and exhale deeply.

By redirecting our focus to our breaths, we momentarily stop our automatic thoughts and are forced to direct attention to each intentional inhalation and exhalation. This conscious awareness to our breath serves to calm our nerves in times of volatility. If you don't believe it, try it for yourselves right now.

This technique has worked for me time and time again. Everytime I catch myself feeling distracted or unhappy, I would stop whatever I was doing, put on my noise cancelling earphones with the music turned off, and to just sit in complete silence as I focused on my breath. After about a minute or two, I find myself with a clearer head. A cleanse of sorts. And then i would attend to whatever task I was doing before.

This takes practice and awareness to be able to do consistently whenever negative emotions rise up. If you feel something is amiss 10x a day, you can carve out 10x of these deep breathing exercises each day as well. Try it and let me know your results.

CPSIA information can be obtained
at www.ICGtesting.com
Printed in the USA
LVHW082056230822
726590LV00014B/514

9 781804 280935